AFFIRMING
CATHOLIC

Helen Stanton

CHRISTIAN
FEMINISM

An Introduction

Series Editor: Jeffrey John

DARTON·LONGMAN+TODD

First published in 1998 by
Darton, Longman and Todd Ltd
1 Spencer Court
140–142 Wandsworth High Street
London SW18 4JJ

in association with

Affirming Catholicism
St Giles Church
No 4, The Postern
Wood Street, The Barbican
London EC2Y 8BJ

ISBN 0–232–52273–1

Designed by Bet Ayer
Phototypeset by Intype London Ltd
Printed and bound in Great Britain by
Page Bros, Norwich

Affirming Catholicism

Affirming Catholicism is a movement (not an ecclesiastical party) which exists to do two things. We affirm our confidence in our Anglican heritage; and we seek to renew and promote the Catholic tradition within it. Our aim is to explore, explain and share with others both inside and outside the Church a lively, intelligent and inclusive Catholic faith. In the words of our Trust Deed:

> It is the conviction of many that a respect for scholarship and free enquiry has been characteristic of the Church of England and of the Churches of the wider Anglican Communion from earliest times, and is fully consistent with the status of those Churches as part of the Holy Catholic Church. It is desired to establish a charitable educational foundation which will be true both to those characteristics and to the Catholic tradition within Anglicanism ... The object of the foundation shall be the advancement of education in the doctrines and the historical development of the Church of England and the Churches of the wider Anglican Communion, as held by those standing within the Catholic tradition.

Our Publications

These are offered as one means of presenting Anglican Catholic teaching and practice in as clear and accessible a form as possible. Some cover traditional doctrinal and liturgical themes; others attempt to present a well-argued Catholic viewpoint on issues of debate currently facing the Church. There is a list of our series of booklets on page v.

The present series of books is provided, where appropriate, with summaries to sections, and suggested questions which we hope will facilitate personal study or discussion in groups. Other titles in the series are:

Catholic Evangelism Stephen Cottrell
Humanity and Healing – Ministering to the Sick in the Catholic Tradition Martin Dudley

To order these publications individually or on subscription, or for further information about the aims and activities of Affirming Catholicism, write to:

The Secretary
Affirming Catholicism
St Giles Church
No 4, The Postern
Wood Street
The Barbican
London EC2Y 8BJ

Tel 0171 638 1980
Fax 0171 638 1997

Books in the Affirming Catholicism series

About the Author

Helen Stanton studied theology at the Universities of Birmingham and Manchester. An Anglican laywoman, she has worked in a variety of Church contexts, including Christian Aid, and as Anglican Chaplain to the University of Sheffield. Currently she is Social Responsibility Officer for the Diocese of Bath and Wells.

She teaches and writes mainly about liberation theologies, including feminist theology, and is Honorary Secretary of the Association of Centres of Adult Theological Education.

Contents

Introduction

For some in the Church of England the ordination of the first women to the priesthood in 1994 marked the end of a struggle within the Church for women to be treated, with men, as those made in the image and likeness of God. Equality has been achieved, they argue, even though it might take time for the implications of women's priesting to be worked out in terms of senior appointments for experienced and appropriate women. Others within the Church have seen the priesting of women as a stage on a journey: for them, only when the episcopate is opened to women will the rightful place of women in the Church have been achieved. For still others the priesting of women has marked the end of the Church's right to be called Catholic and Apostolic.

This short publication is not intended in any way to undermine the achievement of justice and the recognition of God's call to women represented by the decision made by the General Synod on 11 November 1994 and the subsequent ordinations. For me those events were not only landmarks but were occasions of overwhelming rejoicing. What I shall seek to suggest, however, is that the questions which feminism brings to Christian belief and practice are not wholly satisfied by the ordaining of women to the priesthood, and that, even when women are made bishops in the Church of England, feminism will continue to have important and challenging things to say to us.

The place of feminism within Christian theology is a controversial one, and there are theologians, clergy and lay people, for whom feminism is completely unacceptable. The wealth of material being written about and from the perspective of feminist theology, and its almost universal inclusion in academic courses of Theology and Religious Studies, suggests, however, that it should be taken seriously. I believe that the Church should go further, and welcome the insights and enrichment feminist approaches bring to our understanding of the tradition. Yet feminism is also highly critical of aspects of the Christian tradition, and some previously Christian feminists have felt unable to continue as members of the Church in the light of what they perceive. My own position is different, for I believe that the Church is part of a living tradition and can work with that tradition so that it becomes more and more an agent of God's Kingdom, in which the lowly are lifted up and the powerful are overthrown.

This publication introduces some of the major issues within Christian feminist theology: its challenges to the Bible and later tradition, its recovery of female themes and characters, and its reconstruction of theologies that do justice to women. It also looks briefly at the implications of feminist theology for the practice of the Church, and at questions of inclusive language for people and God. Throughout, I shall focus almost exclusively on *Christian* feminist theology, and although I shall highlight some of the concerns about the tradition raised sharply by 'post-Christian' theologians, I shall not discuss the ways in which feminists are engaging with other major religions, nor the relationship between feminism and goddess religions. It is helpful, none the less, to be aware that feminist theology is not an exclusively Christian phenomenon, nor is it simply a concern of western Christians, for feminist, or often womanist,[1] developments are current throughout the worldwide Church, and in the religious world outside it.

The Many Faces of Feminism

Like Christianity, feminism is not a uniform and consistent set of ideas and ideals. Feminist theorists and theologians represent a diversity of standpoints, some of them influenced by wider philosophical or political concerns within which they locate their feminist thinking. Broadly, these diverse standpoints can be divided into three or four main groupings, which I shall attempt to outline here, before drawing some parallels between these groupings and the emphases of feminist theology.

Liberal feminism, following the traditions of Mary Wollstonecraft and John Stuart Mill,[2] generally centres on issues of just practice and equal rights for women and men – for example, the establishment of equal opportunities legislation, of child care provision, and the increased admission of women to professions and educational establishments where women are underrepresented. An example of liberal feminist activity can be seen in the work of the '300 Group', a cross-party organisation to encourage the election of more women to the UK parliament.

Marxist feminism has a primary concern with the economic position of women, seeking to highlight the need for ending women's oppression under capitalism. It also works to put concerns and perspectives which arise from women's experience on the agenda of

Marxist theory, and it seeks to find ways of challenging the patriarchy of Marxism. Marxism has traditionally analysed vested interests specifically in terms of class, but feminist Marxists propose a more complex understanding in which gender and race are also significant. Feminism which has a concern with women's economic position at its core is seen, for example, in women's mobilisation within Trades Unions, and perhaps also in the involvement of the wives of miners in the British miners' strike of 1984. Such movements help to undermine the impression sometimes given that western feminism is a phenomenon which occurs exclusively among middle-class women.

Romantic feminism seeks to affirm what it regards as particularly feminine approaches to life. Unlike some other feminist thinking, this stance emphasises a radical dualism between male and female ways of thinking and being. For example, it often suggests that scientific thought is peculiarly masculine, and that women are allied with nature and with the earth, and are characterised by being in relationship. These aspects of romantic feminism are often prevalent within forms of feminism practised within New Age and goddess-worshipping movements, although not all exponents of romantic feminism espouse goddess worship or Wicce.[3]

Although in its desire to celebrate 'femininity' romantic feminism can seem to resemble understandings of gender which emphasise the complementarity of women and men, in fact it has a very different viewpoint. Most romantic feminists would present the earth, nature and 'feminine' qualities as fundamentally opposed to those of masculinity, and infinitely superior to them. This movement is often, though not necessarily, identified with a radical feminism which may include separatism.

Radical feminism is itself a broad movement including, but not defined by, a separatist standpoint. It is sometimes also, but by no means always, developed by lesbian women. It believes that the oppression of women is the most significant oppression, rather than that of race or class. It makes women's experience its starting-point, and identifies with the slogan 'the personal is the political'. Radical feminism speaks of 'patriarchy', the system of structures and ideologies which reinforce male power and female subordination. Important themes in radical feminism are women's control of their bodies, violence against women, critiques of heterosexuality, and the building up of a sense of sisterhood for the empowerment of women.

Christian feminism
There are some who argue that Christian feminism goes back as far as the ministry of Jesus. I shall examine this claim later. It can certainly be argued that 'feminine' themes are present in the work of visionaries and mystics like Hildegard of Bingen and Julian of Norwich. Women's powerful contribution to the Church is evident in the stories of our best-known women saints, like Teresa of Avila, and by those not so well celebrated in our history, like Mary Ward, Elizabeth Cady Stanton, Maude Royden and many others. In more modern terms, however, the rise of

Christian feminism coincided with what may be called the first wave of feminism in the nineteenth century.[4]

By 1792, Mary Wollstonecraft[5] had already written her central feminist text *The Vindication of the Rights of Women*, in which she asserted the equality of women, recognised their subordination in male-dominated society, and expounded the need for women to share the rights and opportunities of men so that they might gain independence and respect. By the mid nineteenth century feminist insight began to focus around the issue of women's suffrage, and many of those in North America who had organised against slavery began to campaign on behalf of women.

Notable among these were Elizabeth Cady Stanton and Susan B. Anthony who wrote *The History of Women's Suffrage*, and who collaborated later in the century in commissioning *The Women's Bible*. For her persistence with this, Cady Stanton has been called 'probably the first feminist theologian'.[6] Completed in 1895, and renounced by the institutional Churches, *The Women's Bible* consisted of commentary by women biblical and linguistic scholars who examined the biblical texts from a feminine perspective and also pointed to the absence of women from the text. The themes that they highlighted, namely violence and cruelty against women, the invisibility of women in the Bible, and the unquestioned all-pervasiveness of patriarchy in the tradition, are still significant in Christian feminism today.

Some Christian feminist writers see Christian feminism as compatible only with liberal feminism, with its emphasis upon what might be called the gospel imperative for justice. In fact Christian feminists make links with all four of the groupings I have identified, though some are wary of the dangers of stereotyping inherent in romantic feminism. Many Christian feminists see parallels with the work of Marxist feminists in their own attempts to challenge a patriarchal institution and ideology. Most notably, perhaps, Christian feminism has a great deal in common with radical feminism's analysis of patriarchy, suggesting that aspects of Christian doctrine and practice developed, more or less consciously, in the interests of male power and female subordination, giving divine sanction to this order of things. Christian feminism draws upon the neglected experience of women as a key interpretative tool, and, as part of a liberationist approach to theology, seeks to develop an understanding and practice in which women are liberated from oppression and subordination as the Kingdom vision of Jesus comes to be realised.

Womanist theology and feminist theology

Womanist theology also takes themes from radical feminism seriously, but, like Marxist feminism, seeks to set feminist aims within a more complex framework than gender only. Originating amongst African American women theologians, though now also an influence in Latin American theology,[7] this development seeks to address the 'triple jeopardy' of race, poverty and gender. Womanist theologians are frequently very critical of the middle-class origins of feminism and of middle-class concepts of sisterhood, for black women often experience white women as oppressors. The novelist Alice Walker graphically sums up the feminist/womanist divide: 'Feminist is to womanist as lavender is to purple.'[8] Not all women theologians from the two-thirds world reject the term feminism, however, and some Asian, as well as western, theologians question whether womanist theology gives sufficient emphasis to gender oppression.

Can men be feminists?
This frequently asked question finds a variety of answers among feminists. Most feminists believe that men can be, and that some men are, supportive of feminist aims. A glance at the four styles of feminism which I have just outlined suggests much with which men can be in agreement, and for which men can be allies. Many men would, therefore, describe themselves as feminists, and are accepted by women as such.

Other feminists are more hesitant. They are wary of the way in which patriarchy has constantly found ways of controlling women's lives, and are concerned that men who describe themselves as feminists may come to take power within the feminist movement, and find themselves, perhaps unconsciously, defining and directing women's liberation. Among most feminists there is a strong sense that women need to take control of their own liberation, to empower themselves, and provide their own focuses and methods for feminist thinking and action which reflect women's particular experience.

For some feminists, mostly those associated with radical feminism, there is a sense that men have such strong vested interests in patriarchy that they cannot possibly be supportive of feminism. This last stance is very much a minority view, however, and most feminist women think it possible for men to be allies in the changing of the world so that patriarchy may be overcome. Some feminists, taking their cue from those who work against racism, say that the chief task of male feminists is to become aware of, and then to overcome, their own oppressive behaviour. As I have indicated, some male supporters of feminism call themselves feminists, though increasingly, to indicate a recognition that men must not come to dominate feminism, the word 'pro-feminist' is used.

Certainly there are men who have come to realise the power and injustice of patriarchy. They highlight the idea that if the gender stereotyping of women is challenged, then the gender stereotyping of men is automatically called into question, and men too may be liberated from the ways in which patriarchy has constrained them. A very significant book written from this perspective is *Who Needs Feminism*? which consists of articles by some important male theologians mainly from the UK.[9] One contributor, Christopher Rowland, elsewhere hints at an appropriate stance for the male, pro-feminist theologian:

> The full story of radical Christianity would devote a significant place to the creativity and ingenuity of women throughout the centuries to make space for themselves in an institution and culture which rapidly became male dominated. . . . Much valuable work is being done to recover the important role of women as exponents of a submerged but authentic voice of Christian discipleship . . . at this stage [I] do not feel able to improve on the excellent work which is now available from women theologians.[10]

Another important pro-feminist writer is Brian Wren, whose commitment to feminism, and especially to the cause of inclusive language, can be traced through the development of his hymn writing and his issuing of inclusive versions of his early hymns. I will draw upon his book *What Language Shall I Borrow*?[11] in my discussion of inclusive language and the naming of God.

Context and vision

Feminist theology is part of a wider theological movement which is usually described as contextual theology. These theologies recognise that God speaks to humanity through the particularity of experience and that God's calling will not be the same for a rural community in El Salvador and a middle-class congregation in the Home Counties. Contextual theology asserts that all theology is contextual, and that what purports to be 'neutral' theology is usually the theology of those in power, the *status quo*, which would prefer its preconceptions not to be called into question. Like other contextual theologies, feminist theology seeks to expose and examine the vested interests of the *status quo* from its own context, namely from women's perspectives.

Like all contextual theologies, feminist theology is partisan; it seeks to promote empowerment and transformation. In many cases it engages in alliances with other theologies which promote justice and liberation from oppressions. Christian feminists believe that this task is an imperative of the gospel: 'Intellectual and existential faithfulness to our Christian faith is important – and many women show such faithfulness to a high degree – but we also need all powers of discernment to recognise the signs of the spirit working among us in the world and the churches today. The new spirit among women can give Christians great ground for hope.'[12]

Tackling the Bible

In approaching Christianity, feminist theologians begin with the understanding that, at the very least, the tradition reflects the patriarchy of the cultures in which it was developed. Often it is asserted that the Christian tradition has been used to promote patriarchy, and, as I have already indicated, some post-Christian feminists find the tradition so overwhelmingly patriarchal that they feel it must be abandoned. However, since this is a publication specifically about Christian feminism, I want to focus on how feminist theologians who continue to identify themselves with the Christian tradition actually use that tradition.

The starting-point for many feminist theologians in interpreting both the Bible and the later tradition is expressed by the phrase 'the hermeneutics of suspicion'. This suggests that the tradition is not something to be embraced wholeheartedly and unquestioningly, but something of which it might appropriately be asked: 'How does this contribute to women's oppression or subordination?'

Invisibility
One of the ways in which this characteristic suspicion of the tradition expresses itself is in raising questions about the dominance of male figures in the Bible. Of course, many female figures are mentioned in Scripture: Miriam and Deborah and Hannah and the female disciples of Jesus are there, though, more

often, as in the case of many of the women disciples, we do not know their names. However, in comparison with the male figures, with Moses and Aaron, with Joshua and Gideon, with Abraham and Isaac and Jacob and David and Solomon, with Peter and James and John and Paul, the women pale into the background.

When women are represented, frequently their stories are not commonly used in the Church. It is as though the later tradition has marginalised women in the Bible still further. Thus, for example, when I was young everyone who attended a Sunday school was familiar with the story of Joshua, but it was only years later that I discovered Deborah, or indeed had any idea that the Judges of Israel included women.

This failure to teach aspects of the tradition seems to work in relation to both Old and New Testaments. Recently I asked a group of Anglican ordinands to identify twenty women characters in the New Testament without referring to their Bibles. After a little confusion about how many Marys there were, they were able to name twelve. There was no such difficulty with male characters.

Clearly there are important women figures in the New Testament who play significant roles: Mary the mother of Jesus and prophet of the Magnificat; Mary Magdalene, the apostle to the apostles – the first person to proclaim the resurrection; Mary of Bethany and her sister Martha, who receives a bad press in the synoptic Gospels, but who in John's Gospel is the first person to recognise that Jesus is the Christ. There is the girl raised from the dead, the women healed, women with whom Jesus has conversations, and the woman who anoints him, to whom Elizabeth Schussler Fiorenza dedicates her key feminist text *In Memory of Her*. Fiorenza writes:

> While the stories of Judas and Peter are engraved in the memory of Christians, the story of the woman is virtually forgotten. Although Jesus pronounces in Mark, 'and truly I say to you, wherever the gospel is preached in the whole world, what she has done will be told in memory of her' (14:9), the woman's prophetic sign-action did not become a part of the gospel knowledge of Christians. Even her name is lost to us. Wherever the gospel is proclaimed and the Eucharist celebrated another story is told: the story of the apostle who betrayed Jesus. The name of the betrayer is remembered, but the name of the faithful disciple is forgotten because she was a woman.[13]

Many of the women who are recorded in the Gospels are unnamed, including the women disciples who supported Jesus' mission. When we think of Jesus' disciples we think of Peter or Andrew or John. I often meet groups who, though reading their Bibles daily for maybe forty years, suddenly discover the women disciples of Luke's Gospel, having had no conception that a group of women as well as men followed Jesus. The later tradition has made little of these named and nameless women except for the Virgin Mary, and Mary Magdalene, who has frequently been constructed as a 'scarlet woman' in contrast to the Virgin.

Abuses of women and misuse of their stories
Silence about women, or the minimising of the role of the women who are present in our Bibles, is not the only cause of suspicion amongst feminist interpreters. A second concern has centred around

what Phyllis Trible, a leading feminist Old Testament scholar, calls 'documenting the case against women.'[14] Trible herself has been a pioneer in this area, and her book *Texts of Terror*[15] highlights some of the nastiest material about women in the Bible, or indeed anywhere else. A reading of the story of Sodom from the perspective of the treatment of women in the story (Genesis 19:8) and the other texts which Trible focuses upon (Judges 11:29–40; 2 Samuel 13; Judges 19) builds up a picture of horrifying brutality towards women. These texts are extreme cases, but the theme of women's subordination to the interests of men can also be detected in some of the best-known biblical narratives.

Women do play significant roles in the Bible, and yet a closer analysis shows that their contribution is regarded as much less important than that of men. Abraham's faith is a source of celebration in the letter to the Romans, but Sarah is not mentioned. In the Old Testament narratives of the Abraham cycle, Sarah does have a more prominent role, especially in relation to the conception of Isaac and to the casting out of Hagar. Sarah is, however, seen throughout in patriarchal terms, as wife and mother, as defender of her son's inheritance. The rival claims between Isaac and Ishmael divide Sarah from her maid in acts of cruelty which are often analysed in terms of class and race divisions. Sarah is, as it were, an agent of patriarchy – she serves its purposes.

The story of Sarah is one which I have used with groups of women in churches for a number of years now. Often they are less in awe of Abraham as hero of the faith than we are usually taught to be; they ask questions about the 'exemplary' act of preparing his son for sacrifice, and are none too impressed by his passing off Sarah as his sister so that she can be offered for sex to the Pharaoh. The mismatch between the implication of the texts and these Christian women's sense of what it means to love children and partners certainly inculcates a suspicion of the Pauline tradition which congratulates Abraham for offering his son, and fails to denounce his treatment of Sarah. It is as though champions of the faith may entirely disregard and, indeed, endanger wives and children to meet their God's heroic ends.

The book of Ruth is another example of a distortion of the tradition, this time in an apparent attempt to promote romantic love. The book of Ruth is frequently presented as a supreme love story, and indeed it is, though the strength of love is focused between the two women, Ruth and Naomi. The book is primarily about the embodying of God's steadfast love by a person outside the community of faith. The 'love story' between Ruth and Boaz is not at all conventional, since the initiative is Ruth's and she blatantly sets out to seduce him. This emphasis on the stranger as the bearer of God's love, on committed love between women, and a woman's sexual confidence and initiative, is frequently omitted from popular discussions of the book's significance.

Listening for lost voices
If a 'hermeneutic of suspicion' is a starting-point for feminist approaches to the Bible, Christian feminists also take other approaches, for if the tradition were wholly negative about women it would be impossible

to remain with it. But in looking at the way feminist theologians have recovered women-positive aspects of the tradition, it is important not to underestimate the difficulties which still lie within the tradition. The material which feminist theologians use in the processes of recovery and reconstruction is significant because it appears in the biblical texts at all, and its existence against all the odds may perhaps suggest the original existence of a greater wealth of material which was unable to permeate patriarchal exclusion. Schussler Fiorenza speaks of this interpretative process thus: 'Like the woman of the Gospels searching diligently for lost coins, so a hermeneutic of re-vision investigates biblical texts for submerged meanings, lost voices, and authorising visions.'[16]

This process is necessary because theology, like history and politics, is written by those who achieve and sustain power. As Christopher Rowland comments:

> The details of the stories of many of the saints have been submerged for ever beneath an ocean of contrary opinion. It is important to piece together the story of the opponents of the dominant religious ideologies from the hints and fragments available to us. The task of recovery is an arduous one but it is long overdue; we have for too long accepted the story offered by the powerful.[17]

Women's stories

The recovery of the women of the biblical tradition is a significant part of feminist theology. Celebrating those who, despite patriarchy, made a contribution can be greatly affirming of contemporary women, not least those who are themselves marginalised. There are many books by feminist theologians which attempt to make visible the women of the tradition, including Alice Lafferty's exhaustive *Wives, Harlots and Concubines – Women in the Old Testament*,[18] and Elizabeth Moltmann-Wendel's *The Women around Jesus*.[19] Although there may be dangers in celebrating remarkable women who simply make ordinary women feel inadequate, it is important to note that the biblical tradition does find a place for ordinary women: for example, the naming of Shiphrah and Puah, the Hebrew midwives whose refusal to comply with the order to kill Hebrew boys has become an inspiration for the resistance of brutality by other ordinary women.[20]

Highlighting biblical themes

As well as recovering particular women in the story of the people of God, feminism seeks to recover themes in the tradition which suggest that God intends women's place within creation to be very different from that apportioned by patriarchy. One example is the highlighting of the contrasting place of women implied in the two creation stories. In Genesis 2, there is the familiar story of Eve being created from Adam's rib. The male is prime here, and it is only when the other creatures are found to be unsuitable companions for Adam that Eve is created: she is clearly an afterthought and created primarily for Adam. Even so, some interpreters note that the word translated 'helpmeet' or 'helper' in English Bibles is a term used also of God, so that the woman is someone of more significance than English translations suggest. Interpreters also point to the equality indicated by Eve's ability to speak for herself and Adam when talking with the serpent.

None the less Genesis 1 presents a very different picture of woman's place in the creation. The New RSV translates verse 27: 'So God created humankind in his image, in the image of God he created them, male and female he created them.' Although this first chapter of Genesis places humanity in dominion over the rest of the creation, there is clear equality between woman and man; they both bear God's image and there is no sense of woman being either an after-thought or primarily created for man.

This starting-point in Genesis 1 sets a very different tone from much of the tradition and can provide a useful criterion by which the later tradition may be judged. It may be appropriate to ask, for example, of different stories or teachings or doctrines: do they do justice to the concept expressed in Genesis 1 that women are equally created in the image and likeness of God?

The motherhood of God

The biblical tradition reveals other aspects of women's experience in a positive light, though these are often obscured by English translations. Within the writings of the Psalms and the prophets especially, images of God nurturing the people of Israel or undergoing the pains of labour are feminine images clear in the Hebrew but not always in English. Typical examples of biblical texts in this category are: Numbers 11:12; Deuteronomy 32:11; Psalm 22:9–10; Psalm 131:2; Isaiah 31:5, 42:14, 46:3, 49:15, 66:13.[21] It is worth looking at these, not least to see how the feminine forms of the biblical language are sometimes distorted, ensuring the invisibility of the original imagery.

'Feminine' themes in the New Testament

Within the New Testament, feminist approaches to 'feminine' themes are made more complex by the portrayal of the Church as feminine in the Pauline epistles, the letter to the Ephesians[22] and the book of Revelation. Some see these portrayals as reinforcing the subordination of women: if the Church is feminine in relation to Christ as masculine, how can the feminine be anything but subordinate? Other scholars, however, regard this imagery as chiefly concerned with the nature of the Church. In the case of Ephesians, they see the author drawing upon contemporary structures of marriage to illustrate the almost inevitably unequal relationship between Christ and the Church. Nevertheless for a significant number of Christians this text remains one which justifies hierarchy between women and men. This is so for Christians who affirm the value of 'headship', and many feminist writers are critical of Ephesians 5 for its reinforcement of hierarchy within marriage. Rosemary Ruether, who in any case expresses concern about the tradition of a radical difference between God and humanity, is convinced that the author of Ephesians is confused in understanding the Church because the analogy draws upon an 'unrealistic' view of marriage:

> By making the husband analogous to Christ in relation to his wife, the author even suggests that a wife should consider her husband representative of Christ! Her

husband is her Lord, as Christ is Lord of the Church. She is his body, as the Church is the body of Christ.[23]

A second cause of feminist suspicion of the New Testament lies in the lack of feminine imagery to recover. In the Gospels Jesus likens himself to a mother hen, and in the parable of the lost coin God is likened to a woman. A closer look, however, reveals a rather less encouraging picture from a feminist perspective, for it can seem that there is little to challenge patriarchy. Nicola Slee's research into the parables[24] reveals eighteen main characters in Mark's Gospel, all of them men. In Matthew, of eighty-five main characters, twelve are women, but ten of those are bridesmaids; and in Luke, of the one hundred and eight main characters, only nine are women. The recovery of submerged feminine themes in the Gospels is put into perspective by these numbers. As far as the parables are concerned, Slee identifies a 'surface dominance of male characterisation' and 'an anonymity of women'.[25] Such imagery as there is reinforces stereotypes, for:

> The male characters in the parables cover a wide range: farmers, builders, merchants, kings, judges, stewards, doctors, bridegrooms, servants, fathers, priests, publicans, rich men, poor men, thieves, fools, scoundrels and more. The women featured in the parables can be listed exhaustively as: ten bridesmaids, a woman seeking justice, a handful of unspecified wives, mothers and daughters mentioned in general terms (e.g. Matthew 18:23–5, Luke 12:51–3).[26]

None the less Slee highlights the way in which the parables reflect women's bodily and domestic experience, though those experiences are still constrained. For Slee, Jesus' observation of the minutiae of domestic life is an affirming of women: not an acceptance of the restriction of women's lives within the domestic, but a recognition that the everyday is irreversibly transformed as the place of God's activity. For her, the parables show Jesus recognising the limitations of women's lives, expanded by the in-breaking of the Kingdom.

Jesus and women

Very often popular Christian feminist interpretation tries to present a great gulf between the Old and New Testaments with regard to women. Writers and preachers suggest that, while the Old Testament and the culture in which Jesus found himself was thoroughly patriarchal, and while St Paul was influenced by patriarchal thought, Jesus himself took a radically different view. For many Christian feminists, the idea that Jesus himself challenged the patriarchy and gender-stereotyping of his day is a key factor in their continuing Christian identity. They would argue that, at least in his practice, Jesus contributed to the undermining of social conventions in relation to women.

Some are not convinced, however. In her challenging book *Theology and Feminism*, post-Christian feminist Daphne Hampson argues that there is 'not a shred of evidence' that 'Jesus was a feminist'.[27] Hampson assumes that, at the very least, feminism requires a commitment to the equality of men and women, and that although there appears to be evidence that Jesus 'reached out to women as individuals in their need' and that he was not misogynist, there is no evidence that he was committed to gender equality, 'no evidence that he mounted a critique of the position in which women were placed in his society.'[28]

Urging Christians to be aware of the diversity of first century (CE) Judaism, Hampson suggests that in fact 'there was probably nothing particularly exceptional about Jesus' behaviour and attitude towards women.' She draws upon the work of Judith Orschorn, a scholar of the Ancient Near East, in observing that what Jesus represented was already present in various forms of contemporary Judaism.[29]

Hampson compares Jesus' attitude to women with his attitude to the poor, where she believes he was aware of the wider social and structural issues involved. Her view is that Jesus preached the need for revolution in relation to the lives of the poor. Not so in relation to women, says Hampson, where 'There is no positive evidence that Jesus saw anything wrong with the sexism of his day. He did not, as far as we know, see the necessity for structural change to remedy the oppression that women were under.' Nor 'in the realm of religion does Jesus appear to have done anything to counter the inferior position in which women were placed.'[30]

Yet many Christian feminists see signs of a challenge to patriarchy in Jesus' behaviour. He is found speaking with the notorious woman at the well; he chooses a woman to proclaim the resurrection; he shows no sign of distress in breaking a blood taboo when he heals the woman with a haemorrhage. (Indeed, the theological purpose of this miracle appears to be the abolition of the taboo itself.) He heals women and men indiscriminately, and includes women as well as men among his disciples, though not, it is recorded, among the twelve. He is anointed by a woman who may have been a prostitute.

These Christian feminists would argue that Jesus' personal practice may be used as the basis of a visionary challenge within the new community of God's Kingdom which he preached, and that his concern for the liberation of the oppressed might legitimately be applied to those oppressed on the basis of gender. It can be argued that Christian feminism is an appropriate development of his vision of the Kingdom, as are other key areas of doctrine and practice not overt in the Gospels. Hampson's argument is powerful and needs to be taken seriously, but it is not, I believe, necessarily overwhelming.

Interpreting the Later Tradition

Feminist interpretation of the post-biblical Christian tradition uses similar tools to those I have described in relation to biblical material. These include a 'suspicious' approach to the patriarchal nature of much of the tradition, and the recovery of lost voices and characters and the reconstruction of the tradition, in order to do justice to minority themes and to women's current experiences and insights. This publication cannot outline all the areas where these methods are used, but I will briefly outline a few key areas.

Women's bodies

The growing significance of Greek thought within Christianity contributed to an increasingly dualistic understanding of the world. The body and the mind or spirit became radically divided in a way which was largely alien to the culture and understanding of the Old Testament. Within this dualism there was a clear hierarchy, the mind or spirit taking precedence over the body. For the early Church Fathers especially, there were also gender implications, for women were associated with bodiliness in a way that men were not. No doubt influenced by Ancient Near Eastern taboos about menstruation and childbirth, this anthropological dualism reinforced women's subordination to men, for whom commitment to the spiritual life meant rising above their bodiliness.

For those who had ears to hear, aspects of this

belief were evident in the discussions about women and priesthood in the late 1980s. There has been a sense since the early centuries of the Christian faith that women could not be called to leadership within the Church because women were more 'bodily' than men, and unable to leave behind their 'bodiliness' in order to attain the appropriate spiritual heights.

Feminist theologians are suspicious of pronouncements by the powerful in the Church – almost uniformly men – which seem to undermine the value, self-esteem or power of women. Some of the greatest of the Fathers of the Church believed that women were defective men, or that bearing a child was a passive process in which only the male seed was an active force. These statements may have been based on the biological understandings of the time, but their implications for women have remained long after biological understandings have been revised.

Some feminists have sought to reinterpret this emphasis upon women's bodies and have drawn upon bodily experience in developing new theologies, as in Janet Morley's prayers:

> God our beloved,
> born of a woman's body,
> you came that we might look upon you,
> and handle you with our own hands.
> May we so cherish one another in our bodies
> that we may also be touched by you;
> through the Word made flesh, Jesus Christ, Amen.[31]

Invisibility
It may seem improbable for a Catholic Anglican to suggest that women are invisible in the tradition. A

glance at any 'lives of the saints' would indicate otherwise. I would suggest, however, that it is also plain from a glance at the female saints' hagiographies that only certain clearly-defined types of women have been made visible within the Church. It is significant that we have only *Fathers* of the Church, and that although there were notable exceptions, men dominated theology until the second half of this century. Janet Morley draws attention to the gender of saints listed in *The Alternative Service Book*. She notes the recording of sixty-six men but only ten women in the calendar of lesser saints, and goes on to draw some interesting distinctions between the ways female and male saints are portrayed: 'The celibate Francis of Assisi is just a "Friar", but Clare is specifically a "Virgin". Josephine Butler is a "Social Reformer, Wife and Mother", while William Wilberforce is simply a "Social Reformer".' Morley asks: 'Why is sexual practice and marital status significant in a woman's vocation, and not a man's?'[32] Among the most significant of saints Morley detects 'a further difference: Catherine of Siena, Teresa of Avila and John of the Cross, all learned spiritual writers, are each described as "Mystics", but only the man has the distinction of being called "Teacher of the Faith".'

It may well be that it was the association of women with heretical groups which contributed to the marginalisation of women within orthodox Christianity, though it might also be argued that the very power of women within these groups contributed to their ostracism by a patriarchal Church. Writers such as Elaine Pagels, whose book *The Gnostic Gospels*[33] explores these themes in earliest Christianity, Elizabeth Moltmann-Wendel and others, see the dominance of the Virgin Mary within the tradition, rather than Mary Magdalene, as a part of a patriarchal process. In the Gnostic Gospels Mary Magdalene is a significant figure, a friend and companion of Jesus, at least equal to the apostles. Both Pagels and Moltmann-Wendel speculate that patriarchal orthodoxy suppressed this tradition of a uniquely powerful woman.

The omission of many women from the tradition has continued. Important figures like twentieth-century preacher Maude Royden are almost unknown. It also seems to be possible, even now, in our theological colleges and courses for reading lists to be drawn up on major doctrinal themes which entirely omit the writings of women. Although women may not have been able to train in theology in the same way as men until the end of the nineteenth century, that is not the case now, and the omission of the contributions of major women theologians may play a significant part in maintaining patriarchy.

Virgin martyrs
While feminists have been suspicious of the tradition, there has also been a process of recovery similar to that exercised in relation to biblical studies, though again it has not been an uncritical recovery. In the Catholic tradition, the celebration of women saints has been part of regular liturgical practice. Feminist theologians, however, would ask what sorts of messages about 'holy women' are conveyed through the women we celebrate. The great emphasis upon virgin martyrs who resisted marriages despite torture

and death may express some very negative beliefs about women and sexuality, and about disregard for women's bodies in comparison with the life of the spirit. The virgin martyrs attain the spiritual affirmation of the Church by, as it were, accepting the dualism of the Church and heroically denying what the Church rejects as unspiritual.

Of course men did likewise, for the great male saints of the medieval Church were uniformly celibate. Yet as Morley shows, by and large these saints are remembered and celebrated for something else: many may have been virgins, but they are primarily remembered as scholars. They may have been martyrs, but for the most part they did not die defending their virginity. With the notable exception of the second century Origen, who, according to tradition, castrated himself 'for the sake of the Kingdom', the Church does not tell in gory detail the torture and mutilation men endured defending their 'purity'.

It is possible to view virginity, and perhaps especially vowed virginity within the context of the religious life, as one of the ways in which women could acquire a degree of autonomy and independence. The more powerful of these women, reformers and visionaries like Teresa of Avila and Catherine of Siena, were models of a different way of life for women, and those who were involved in the education of girls may be seen as helping to improve the general status of women. However, it could also be argued that the great gulf which lay between the lives of religious women and ordinary women served to undermine the self-esteem of the latter.

Celebrating women

Feminist celebration of women in the tradition has identified a vast number of other significant figures who for a variety of reasons had been lost. It is notable that Julian of Norwich was only 'recovered' early in this century, and, though this was not from any feminist motivation, her disappearance may have had something to do with her visions of Christ as mother. Until recently, a prolific writer and composer like the polymath Hildegard of Bingen was uncelebrated outside Germany, despite her extraordinary influence during her lifetime. Likewise, our understanding of the tradition is being enriched by knowledge of the Béguines, Mechtild of Magdeburg, Gertrude of Halfta, Mechtild of Hackenborn, Elizabeth of Schönnau, and other mystical women who were virtually unknown except to medieval scholars.

Alongside the towering, and sometimes intimidating, heroines of the faith, there were very many other women whose contribution was significant but who have been forgotten. Lavinia Byrne, in a series of books which make a unique contribution to the recovery of forgotten women in the Christian tradition,[34] tells the stories of women preachers, wives and mothers who were also spiritual directors or missionaries, women who cared for the poor and who campaigned against structural injustice. All these are, Christian feminists would argue, worthy of attention and celebration, not least for demonstrating the tenacity and courage of those struggling to forward the Kingdom while frequently opposed by the Church.

Recovering Our Lady

For a significant number of feminist theologians the mother of Jesus has become such a powerful figure for the purposes of patriarchy that she can contribute nothing to the empowerment of women. Indeed, in the view of some writers, she must be abandoned as the central female icon of the Christian faith and be superseded by Mary Magdalene. This is not, however, the only response which feminist theologians make to Mary. For many feminist writers from both Catholic and Protestant traditions the reconstruction of Mary has become a key task, something attested by the great wealth of material currently being published about her.

As with feminist approaches to the Bible, the feminist approach to Mariology involves the process first of uncovering patriarchal influences in the traditions which surround Mary, and secondly the reinterpretation of the tradition so that she becomes an icon for the empowerment of women. Feminist writers like Marina Warner[35] argue that the Marian tradition has been especially directed and guarded by patriarchy. Patriarchal self-interest constructs, from the little that we know of Mary from the Gospels, an icon who reinforces feminine stereotypes of nurturing and maternity, while at the same time undermining women's self-esteem by presenting them with the impossible ideal of virgin motherhood. Indonesian theologian Marianne Katoppo puts this starkly: 'Statues or paintings usually depict her as sugar-sweet, fragile, with eyes either modestly downcast or upturned to heaven – not quite here-and-now! Such a presentation of Mary is, of course, an extremely useful means of domesticating women and other oppressed people.'[36]

Attempts to work with Mary within a feminist framework are not limited to those belonging to Catholic and Orthodox traditions, since, for an increasing number of Protestants, the very absence of Mary from their tradition is seen as part of a patriarchal distortion of the faith. For these Protestant women the language of recovery to which I have referred earlier is especially appropriate, for Mary had been all but lost. Korean theologian Chung Hyun Kyung summarises this position from her own context: 'Asian women think that the Protestant tradition's repudiation of Mariology and its imposition of an all-male theology shows the church's "avoidance of responsibility to address women's place in realistic terms" . . . If the Protestant church has succeeded in oppressing women by eliminating Mary, the Catholic church has exercised control over women by domesticating Mary.'[37]

The sugar-sweet Mary is one with whom many of us were brought up, but who has been experienced by many women as an inadequate image of womanhood made in the image and likeness of God. Roman Catholic Sister Celine Mangan describes the cause of this inadequacy which many Catholic women have perceived: 'Mary as the immaculate model of purity was put forward as the ideal of young womanhood in our young days, but an ideal which was modelled on the rather cold anaemic statues of Mary which were prevalent at that time, rather than on the real full-blooded woman of Nazareth.'[38]

Although, as I have indicated, some Christian feminists, both Protestant and Catholic, believe that Mary does not help the cause of women and that she is so badly contaminated by patriarchy that she must be discarded or at the very least marginalised,[39] other feminist theologians have recognised Mary's potential. They have perceived in her an icon capable of being remade for women's empowerment.

This movement to rework Mary uses a literary approach to the relatively scant material about Mary in the Bible, which involves an imaginative, almost Ignatian, entering into the story. This methodology is not confined to the West, and has produced some powerful creative writing. Korean theologian Kuk Yum begins to describe the Visitation in the voice of Mary: 'I was afraid to meet people's eyes and even Joseph's. However, as soon as I met Elizabeth, my fear was suddenly gone.'[40] Kuk Yum continues to use Mary's voice to reflect upon the Visitation as an example of the feminist concept of sisterhood: 'To accomplish a certain task there should be solidarity of similar-minded people, like the solidarity Elizabeth and I had. Solidarity is an important fact of forming and enriching community. Solidarity, sisterhood, does not arise of itself.'[41]

There is also a dynamic interpretation of Mary to which the Magnificat is key. As the prophet of the Magnificat, Mary is seen to embody the overthrow of the mighty, and by implication the patriarchal Marian tradition, and she becomes instead an icon of the poor who are lifted up in the Kingdom of God. Thus the Magnificat becomes a framework used to justify the wholesale rejection of the tradition of Mary as a passive, obedient woman, and the reconstruction instead of a Mary who is in solidarity with the poor.

This feminist approach to Mary bears some resemblance to that of Latin American liberation theology.

The use of the Magnificat has resulted in the creation of Mary as an image of women in the struggle for justice, especially in the work of two-thirds world feminist theologians. For them Mary becomes a poor person, not to make the *status quo* bearable by her comforting presence, but in order to empower the poor and especially poor women. There are very many examples of this reconstruction of Mary throughout the world. Katoppo gives an example which she contrasts with the tradition she regards as oppressive:

> Asian Catholics, for example, are beginning to see her no longer as the 'fairy queen oozing out sweet piety', but rather as 'the mature and committed (Asian) woman, the peasant mother who cheerfully wears herself out to feed and clothe her carpenter son; the worker's wife wearing holy furrows on her face . . .an image reflected in millions of Asian village mothers today.'[42]

Some western feminists see this image of Mary as a politically pacifying one, but this underestimates the effects of increased self-esteem and consequent empowerment in the process whereby 'the most holy lady on the pedestal comes down, wears dirty clothing and empowers the poor as one of them.'[43] Chung and Mapa report that:

> This radical servanthood of Mary was witnessed in the 'people power' of the Philippines, which forced the Marcos regime to collapse in 1987. . . .the people of the Philippines carried the huge picture and statue of Mary all through their demonstrations in order to sustain their faith and be empowered by her strength.[44]

Feminism and the Language of Worship

Liturgy frequently elicits very strong feelings and produces some fierce disagreements. This is scarcely surprising, for cultural, aesthetic, doctrinal and personal factors all play their part in relation to worship. The Preface to *The Alternative Service Book* asserts that 'Christians are formed by the way in which they pray, and the way they choose to pray expresses what they are.'[45]

Feminist theologians criticise the language of the liturgy in two main areas, both of which are sometimes indicated by the phrase 'inclusive language', though the term does not necessarily imply both these areas. The first concerns human beings, and especially the use of masculine nouns and pronouns in ways which are claimed to 'include' or 'exclude' women. The second concerns feminine imagery for God. Both these areas are capable of arousing very strong feelings. I will consider them separately.

Man includes woman?

Feminist theology shares with other feminist writings a critique of the effects of using 'men' to indicate men and women and 'he' to mean he and she. Feminists regard the so-called generic use of 'man' as helping to create and perpetuate women's invisibility. The Church has lagged behind society generally in relation to the use of inclusive language. Does this show a proper reluctance to 'conform to the spirit of the age'? Or is it a failure on the Church's part to ally itself with a movement for justice which is part of our Christian calling?

I have already indicated that one of the key focuses of feminism and feminist theology is the need to take women's experience seriously within the tradition. The use of inclusive language, enabling women to be named alongside men as part of the living tradition of the Church, has increasingly become a significant part of a movement to make women visible. Some sympathetic male Church leaders have even experimented with the use of 'women' to mean men and women in order to help themselves and their congregations to recognise the effect which inclusive language has upon women.

In response to feminist critique in this area many Churches have amended their liturgy, more or less formally, so that the Creed is adapted to read 'for us and for our salvation' (instead of 'for us *men*'), and, more rarely, that Christ 'was made human' (instead of 'was made *man*'). Very commonly the Confession is changed to 'we have sinned against you and against our neighbour' (instead of 'against our *fellow men*'). The Report of the Liturgical Commission of the General Synod of the Church of England *Making Women Visible*[46] includes a list of possible adaptations for passages in the *ASB* which are felt to exclude women. The Roman Catholic Church also discourages the use of exclusive, generic terms and suggests alternatives.

For some who lead worship and for others within

congregations, these developments are a source of offence. Others tolerate them but see inclusive language as a compassionate response to a problem of women's oversensitivity. Among those for whom the drive to use inclusive language is anathema, Janet Morley detects two fundamentally contradictory reactions.[47] On the one hand, it may be argued that the issue is trivial – it is seen as making a fuss about nothing. On the other, especially if inclusive language is adopted, instead of being a fuss about nothing, it may be attacked almost as demonic – an abandonment of 'tradition' or 'Scripture' in capitulation to 'the spirit of the age'.

One of the Churches which has most enabled inclusive language in the UK is the Methodist Church, whose recent hymn-book *Hymns and Psalms* not only seeks to offer new inclusive hymns, using a small amount of feminine imagery for God as well as inclusive words for human beings, but also changes the wording of some hymns. In *Hymns and Psalms* John Mason Neill's Christmas hymn 'Good Christian men, rejoice' becomes 'Good Christians all, rejoice'.[48] There may be questions here about the integrity of the words of the original author, but the editors of *Hymns and Psalms* defend their controversial actions: 'Textual alterations have been made only where these could be pastorally as well as editorially sanctioned'[49] and:

> As far as possible the compilers have endeavoured to offer hymnody which takes equal account of the place of both women and men in the life of the Church, so that no one may be inhibited by insensitive editing from

making a full offering of herself or himself in God's service.[50]

Making Women Visible acknowledges the sensitivity of language changes and 'does not view the report as fixing a definitive position about correct use.' It notes that 'The English language is in a continuous process of change'[51] and takes seriously feminist criticisms of language which excludes women. It is not prescriptive, however:

> The commission itself is not of one mind on which changes are necessary or helpful. The aim of this response is to help the Church of England explore this issue. It also sets out recommendations on how the text of the ASB may best be adapted *where this is felt to be appropriate*.[52]

Making Women Visible also suggests some supplementary texts which seek:

> ...to draw on feminine imagery in scripture and tradition so as to allow the force of such imagery to be felt without going beyond scripture in any way that is controversial or speculative. Verses of scripture have been included in which it is women who are addressed as representatives of our common humanity.[53]

Feminine imagery for God is also included.

The use of inclusive language is often criticised for its clumsiness and lack of poetry. One solution might be to retain ancient and beautiful prayers and hymns, despite their uninclusive male language, but to 'balance' them by the use of hymns and prayers which use uninclusive female nouns and pronouns. It may also sometimes be appropriate informally to change the repeated use of, for example 'brothers' in a hymn, to a balance of 'brothers' and 'sisters', rather than to seek a gender-neutral word.

Naming God

The other issue which falls within the framework of inclusive language is the naming of God. I have already indicated the way in which feminist biblical scholars have uncovered the hidden feminine imagery for God in biblical tradition. Starting with this feminine biblical imagery, feminist and pro-feminist writers have developed significant liturgical and devotional material in which God is named using feminine images or feminine pronouns. Some more traditional writers also make contributions in this area. One of the most successful additions to *Hymns and Psalms* is, for example, Rupert Davies' additional verse to Joachim Neander's hymn translated by Catherine Winkworth, 'Praise to the Lord, the Almighty, the King of Creation', though he avoids the feminine pronoun:

> Praise to the Lord, who doth nourish thy life and
>   restore thee,
> Fitting thee well for the tasks that are ever before
>   thee,
> Then to thy need
> He like a mother doth speed,
> Spreading the wings of grace o'er thee.[54]

Kathy Galloway of the Iona Community offers another example, taking her cue from the fact that 'spirit' in Hebrew is a feminine pronoun. Her Pentecost hymn 'Enemy of Apathy' begins with an image of creation: 'She sits like a bird brooding on the water' and moves through the Johannine idea of the Spirit as interpreter, avoiding the stereotyping implicit in much imagery of motherhood and God. Galloway creates strong images from the biblical story of Pentecost:

> She dances in fire, startling her spectators,
> Waking tongues of ecstasy where dumbness reigned;
> She weans and inspires all whose hearts are open,
> Nor can she be captured, silenced or restrained.[55]

Brian Wren suggests that exclusively masculine imagery for God, such as King, Lord, Father, is a distortion which affects our understanding and knowledge of God. If God is not exclusively male (as the tradition tells us God is not) an exclusive use of male imagery denies us access to important aspects of God. Wren also asserts that naming God in solely masculine terms undermines the position of women 'since it suggests that women are unfit or less fit than men to represent the beauty and greatness of God in language.'[56]

Naming God in exclusively male terms is not only unjust and untrue to the biblical tradition, it is also untrue to the later tradition of the Church. Carolyn Walker Bynam gives a list of over thirty mediaeval saints, writers and theologians who used feminine imagery for various persons of the Trinity, including Anselm, Bernard, Albert the Great, Bonaventure, Aquinas, Richard Rolle, Dante, Catherine of Siena and Margery Kempe, as well as Julian of Norwich.[57]

Just as a tradition of women within the Bible is being uncovered, so the presence of feminine imagery for God is being reclaimed within the work of familiar writers. Prayers like that of St Anselm of Canterbury are gaining increasing popularity:

> And you, my soul, dead in yourself,
> run under the wings of Jesus your mother
> and lament your griefs under his feathers.
> Ask that your wounds may be healed,
> and that, comforted, you may live again.[58]

It is worth noting, however, that not all feminine imagery is feminist either in content or intention. It could be argued that the overwhelming use of maternal images, for example by mediaeval writers, stereotyped the feminine, and was often accompanied by misogynistic practice.

Contemporary feminist and pro-feminist writers frequently move beyond maternal imagery for God, though they include some satisfying examples of gender balancing, as in Jim Cotter's Lord's Prayer:

> Father and Mother of us all,
> Loving God, in whom is heaven . . .[59]

Some Christians have successfully attempted to eradicate gender from their talk of God altogether. A one-time spiritual director of mine spent two years training himself always to refer to God as God not him. Others, though not often in large congregational worship, try to balance 'he' with 'she', shifting from one to the other, in an attempt to create some sense of balance but to preserve the personal in relation to God.

Janet Morley warns against simply substituting nouns and pronouns, and of the potential danger of creating an 'Almighty Mother'. She shows how a deeper exploration of feminine imagery can expand our understanding of God. Morley's work, which is greatly influenced by the imagery of Scripture, is some of the most inventive and powerful. In the psalm, 'I will praise God, my beloved', she makes explicit another theme common from the mystical tradition, namely the integration of sexuality with love for God.

> I will praise God, my Beloved,
> for she is altogether lovely.
>
> Her presence satisfies my soul;
> she fills my senses to overflowing
> so that I cannot speak.
>
> Her touch brings me to life;
> the warmth of her hands makes me wholly alive.
>
> Her embrace nourishes me, body and spirit;
> every part of my being responds to her touch.
>
> The beauty of her face is more than I can bear;
> in her gaze I drown.[60]

Critics of feminist liturgy often point out the sexual nature of some writings, as if sexuality were something pertaining specifically to feminine imagery, and as though the norm of male imagery were not also potentially sexual. This criticism also fails to recognise the eroticism of much traditional material, not least in the Song of Songs, but also in mediaeval writings where either Jesus or Mary may be objects of passionate devotion.

In the area of naming God, considerable concern is expressed about a possible link between addressing

God as feminine and pre-Christian goddess-worship. For many post-Christian feminists the worship of female pagan deities has indeed been a rich vein of exploration, but from a Christian viewpoint, as Morley comments: 'If it is argued that female metaphors for God necessarily imply a sexually female deity (a "goddess"), then male terms would imply a sexually male deity (a "god")...the Judeo-Christian tradition has repeatedly opposed either conception.'[61]

The use of inclusive language for people and for God is likely to continue to provoke strong reactions. For at least some Christians, however, being open to these influences from the tradition has proved a creative and enriching experience for their thinking and devotion.

Feminism and Ministry

During the women priests debate in the Church of England, arguments between those for and against women priests focused on what effect they would have on the nature of the Church and the priesthood. Those in favour of women priests often suggested that if women were priested there would be no significant change, while those against often spoke of the thin end of the wedge which would lead to goddess worship, and a radical and undesirable transformation of the Christian faith and of the Church as we know it. Some of those in favour of women priests quietly agreed that some aspects of this transformation would indeed take place, but regarded it as a transformation consonant with the gospel.[62]

There is a danger of stereotyping in an analysis which suggests women will radically alter the Church, for it is often accompanied by the suggestion that women are not only more nurturing – in the women priest debate this was often emphasised in terms of women's 'natural' affinity to the pastoral role – but are also more co-operative, democratic and more community-conscious. That all women are not like this is obvious from a simple survey of recent women political leaders across the world! Likewise, many male priests and laymen are outstanding examples of a loving, vulnerable and non-hierarchical approach to ministry.

Susan Parsons, when Principal of the East Midlands

Ministry Training Scheme, an ecumenical course for mature ordinands, noted a substantial element of sex-role stereotyping in the ministry which women were expected to exercise: 'One woman is welcomed into her new Parish with an anticipation of the gentle and kindly touch she will bring to ministry; another is "useful" for the way in which she soaks up the emotional stress and pain of parishioners; another is valued for being caring without being "too emotional", yet another is criticised for not being "pastoral".'[63] Parsons comments that 'women who do not fit these preconceived expectations, who question existing social organisation, whose vision may be prophetic, will have a confidence "problem" in relating to the structures supporting these stereotypes.'[64]

While it is important to avoid this sort of stereotyping, the embracing and highlighting of women's experience and insight is likely to have some effect. The empowering of women may work within the Church to challenge the theological basis of women's oppression, not least in relation to hierarchical dualism.

As I indicated at the beginning of this book, the questions which feminism raises about the Christian faith and the practice of the Church are not answered by the ordination of women, significant though that has been for Anglican and other Churches. Nor has the ordination of women to the priesthood within the Church of England been unproblematic for the women involved. Many women priests continue to be faced with prejudices within their congregations, in the wider Church, and among colleagues.

Women priests have told me of being forbidden to

preside at the Eucharist when menstruating, as though this were somehow unclean. One woman, in considerable distress, told me that when she informed her incumbent, a strong supporter of women's ordination, that she and her husband intended to start a family, he declared that he couldn't have a pregnant woman behind the altar.

It is not only Anglican women who face these responses. Despite the fact that the first Congregational woman completed her studies for ordained ministry in 1917, that the first woman Baptist minister was appointed in 1918, and the Methodist Church decided to ordain women to Presbyteral ministry in 1974, prejudices and injustices surrounding women's ministry have not ceased in those denominations either. Indeed, in 1995, the Methodist Church's Commission on Women Presbyters and the Church published a report, *The Cry of the Beloved*, which attempted to highlight some of the experiences of Methodist women ministers during the last twenty years, and called British Methodism to take seriously wider feminist issues.

For Anglican women priests as for ministers of other denominations, while there are problematic experiences, the attitudes of some of their most entrenched opponents have been changed through encountering women's priesthood. The overall picture can be seen as positive. As *The Tablet*'s editorial on 4 January 1997 comments: 'Statistics are never the whole story, particularly within Christian bodies where quality is what counts, but at least it seems a safe deduction that the ordination of women by the Church of England has not had the adverse effects predicted by some commentators, but may rather have been an attraction.'[65]

The effects which Anglican women's priesthood will have upon the Church and priesthood will continue to unfold. It may be that women will bring a particular style and particular gifts to their ministry as priests. What is important is that the Church should enable this to develop without prejudging or proscribing what may evolve.

Feminism and laywomen

Before ordination was a possibility for Anglican women, opportunities for 'professional' lay ministry developed, enabling women to serve, for example, as university and industrial chaplains, and frequently to bring to those roles fresh energies and insights. Immediately following the ordination of women to the priesthood, many laywomen felt these opportunities were becoming less available to them. More recently, however, the decline in vocations to ordination seems to be reversing this tendency. None the less, women's ordination as priests has raised issues sharply for laywomen about the distinctiveness of lay vocation, and groups of laywomen and men have begun to meet to reflect upon the particularity of God's call to the laity.

If at the core of feminism is a challenge to dualism and hierarchy, it is likely that feminism[66] will prove a challenge to those who seek to maintain a strict division between sacred and secular, and perhaps also between lay vocations and ordained and religious vocations. The experience of solidarity in struggling for women's priesthood has meant for some a continuing sense of sisterhood across the lay/ordained division, though some laywomen in particular have felt rejected by ordained women concerned primarily to explore their priestly status.

Despite the encouragement of women's ordination, many feminists would argue that the Church has much to do to honour, celebrate and make visible its laywomen. Writing after the ordination of Methodist women to Presbyteral ministry, Pauline Webb raised some questions which might apply to any denomination: '...what kind of partnership do we share "in the gospel"? Is it a partnership both in the vestry and the kitchen, both in the pulpit and in the pew, both in the council and in the congregation? Or is it the former in each case being dominated by the men and the latter mainly occupied by the women?'[67] Some of these barriers are already breaking down, and in the significantly rural diocese where I currently work, I am not at all surprised to encounter two women church wardens in the parishes I visit, though very often it is still women who dominate the tea and lunch-making.

At both institutional and local levels, feminists argue, there are challenges to be made in the attitudes of the Churches to women. In 1988 the World Council of Churches declared an Ecumenical Decade of Churches in Solidarity with Women, as a way of highlighting women's lives and celebrating women's varied contributions to the life of the world. All women, not just Church women, were to be thus celebrated. Important international conferences have been held throughout the world, and in many countries in the two-thirds world, regional and local groups have raised awareness, and organised and campaigned about issues relating to women's lives. In the UK the impact of the Ecumenical Decade has been minimal and most of the clergy and lay people whom I meet are completely ignorant of it. It is, I believe, significant that a call to reflect upon and support women's lives has been so neglected.

We have much to celebrate about the contribution which women have made and do make to our neighbourhoods and Churches. Yet organisations like the Mothers' Union, the Women's Institute and Townswomen's Guilds continue to be the butt of jokes, despite their involvement in valuable community action, and their courageous addressing of issues, like prostitution, which the Churches often choose to ignore.

Many of our congregations number a majority of elderly women, who because of their prevalence are often undervalued. Christian feminists call us to celebrate these women as God's beloved daughters, whose years of prayer and Bible study make them a significant resource for the Church. Feminists long for a transformation of the Church, not simply in order to promote a few women into positions of power, but rather in order that ordinary women may be recognised and empowered to live to their full potential in God's service.

Re-visioning Christianity

This Introduction to some of the major themes of contemporary Christian feminist theology has, I hope, indicated some of the breadth of the thinking, changing and doing which is the experience of Christian feminism today. This breadth provides a helpful self-critical element within feminist conversation.

Within an Anglican context it is fair to note that not only has the ordination of women to the priesthood failed to destroy the Church, but it is overwhelmingly regarded within and outside the Church of England as a positive development and an enriching of the Church's priesthood.

Christian feminist reflection has, however, begun to transform the Church in other ways also. Feminist theology is now firmly established as essential to the curriculum of academic theology. It is also frequently a source of great creativity, breathing into both popular and academic theology new energy as well as new challenges. The classic liberation theology of Latin America is experiencing something of this, gaining not only a new lease of life through the development of feminist and *mujerista* ('womanist') theology, but a fresh focus and direction. It is one of the great joys of Christian feminist theology that so much of it comes from the two-thirds world: a sign, perhaps, of God's preferential option for the poor.

The influences of Christian feminist theology are not only to be felt in higher education or the two-thirds world. The attention of churches in the UK to language, and the flourishing of new prayers and liturgies from feminist and pro-feminist writers and communities, have made a significant contribution to the prayer of the Church, to its appreciation of the tradition and to its understanding of the nature of God. In broadening understanding in this way, Protestants and Catholics have shared in the process of reclaiming the tradition, of expanding our knowledge, both challenging and celebrating, as appropriate, what is revealed.

As the Church has begun to challenge injustices practised against women as part of its wider commitment to justice, many women have felt a greater sense of their experience being understood and their contribution welcomed. None the less it is important to acknowledge that for some people the increasing influence of Christian feminism upon the Church is painful and uncomfortably disturbing. Questioning and conflict are inevitable companions of profound change, and the Church needs help in living with them, but they are signs of life. The insights of Christian feminism are now an unavoidable part of the Christian landscape. They provide some of the means by which the gospel is being made known, and through which the lives of women and men are being transformed into the likeness of Christ.

As I have indicated throughout this Introduction, the task of feminism is far from complete. This is not surprising. Christianity is a visionary faith, which looks and acts and prays towards what the New Testament calls the Kingdom, or the Reign, of God.

Feminism is, I believe, a part of that vision and a leading light on the way.

Questions

The Many Faces of Feminism

1. What aspects of feminist theology and practice do you perceive to be particularly at work in the contemporary Church? Why do you think these have become significant at this time?

2. How far do you think qualities which are called feminine and masculine apply to the women and men you know? Do you think that these are qualities with which people are born, or are they something taught by parents and society?

3. Are womanist theologians right in arguing for a broader perspective from which to view the oppression of groups and individuals? Why/why not?

4. Feminism seeks to expose the vested interests of patriarchy, which it claims are contrary to the gospel. Are there vested interests within feminism of which you are suspicious? What are they? How do they measure against the message of the gospel?

Tackling the Bible

1. How should the Church respond to biblical texts which treat women as less fully human than men?

2. What action could Churches take to celebrate more fully the whole range of women in the Bible?

3. How convincing do you find Daphne Hampson's

claim that Jesus was not especially radical in his attitude to women? How would you defend your view?

4. How far do you think it is possible to have a suspicious attitude to the Bible while maintaining an orthodox faith?

Interpreting the Later Tradition
1. What do you think lies behind the Church's distrust of the physical through the centuries? Are there things about being physical you would want the Church to celebrate, and why? What, if any, aspects of the Bible and the later Church tradition might help the Church to celebrate these things?

2. Make a list of the women saints who have most influenced you, and of the women you know whom you most admire. What in their stories has most inspired you?

3. What strengths and what problems do you see in feminist reinterpretations of Our Lady? Are there important aspects of traditional Mariology which feminist interpreters have ignored? What are they? Why are they important?

Feminism and the Language of Worship
1. Why are Churches being encouraged to take seriously the use of inclusive language?

2. What has your experience been of inclusive language? Are you convinced by arguments for it to be widely adopted?

3. Read Psalm 22:9–10, 131:2, Isaiah 31:5, which make

use of mothering images for God. What might these sorts of images add to our understanding of the Trinity?

4. Try using feminine imagery for God in some of your prayers for a few days, perhaps using a book of prayers which particularly highlights this theme. How do you feel when you use these prayers? How do they affect your praying? Are they helpful or unhelpful? How do they affect your understanding of God?

Feminism and Ministry
1. What differences might it be making to women, and men, to see a woman presiding at the Eucharist?

2. Have you observed differences in the styles of ministry adopted by women and men? If so, how would you describe those differences?

3. What outcomes might there be for the Church if women are regarded as especially suited to pastoral roles? What effects might this have upon men?

4. How far has the ordination of women to priesthood undermined the ministry and calling of laywomen? How might the Church foster laywomen's vocations?

Notes and References

1. I will make clear this distinction later.
2. J.S. Mill, *On the Subjection of Women* (1869).
3. See Starhawk, 'Witchcraft and Women's Culture' in C. P. Christ and J. Plaskow (eds.), *Womanspirit Rising* (San Francisco: Harper and Row, 1979).
4. The second wave is usually traced to the late 1950s and in the English-speaking world to the publication of Betty Friedan's *The Feminine Mystique* in 1963.
5. 1759–97.
6. S. Dowell and L. Hurcombe, *Dispossessed Daughters of Eve* (London: SPCK, 1981), p. 24.
7. Where the distinction is made between *feminista* and *mujerista* theology.
8. A. Walker, *In Search of Our Mothers' Gardens* (London: The Women's Press, 1984), p. xi.
9. R. Holloway (ed.), *Who Needs Feminism?* (London: SPCK, 1991).
10. C. Rowland, *Radical Christianity* (Cambridge: Polity Press, 1988), p. 10.
11. B. Wren, *What Language Shall I Borrow?* (London: SCM, 1989).
12. U. King, 'Women and Christianity' in T. Elwes (ed.), *Women's Voices* (Marshall Pickering, 1992), p. 158.
13. E. S. Fiorenza, *In Memory of Her* (London: SCM, 1983), p. xiii.
14. P. Trible, 'Feminist Hermeneutics and Biblical Studies' in A. Loades (ed.), *Feminist Theology: A Reader* (London: SPCK, 1990), p. 24.
15. P. Trible, *Texts of Terror* (Philadelphia: Fortress Press, 1984).
16. E. S. Fiorenza, *Searching the Scriptures* (London: SCM, 1993), p. 11.
17. Rowland, op.cit, pp. 1–2.

18. Alice Lafferty, *Wives, Harlots and Concubines – Women in the Old Testament* (London: SPCK, 1990).

19. Elizabeth Moltmann-Wendel, *The Women Around Jesus* (London: SCM, 1982).

20. Exodus 1:15.

21. See Women's Guild Panel on Doctrine of the Church of Scotland, *The Motherhood of God* (Edinburgh: St Andrew Press, 1984), p. 68.

22. Some scholars suggest that Ephesians should not be attributed to Paul.

23. R. Ruether, *Sexism and God-Talk* (London: SCM, 1983), p. 141.

24. N. Slee, 'Parables and Women's Experience' in *MC* 26:2 (1984), pp. 20–31.

25. Ibid., p. 26.

26. Ibid., p. 26.

27. D. Hampson, *Theology and Feminism* (Oxford: Basil Blackwell, 1990), p. 87.

28. Ibid.

29. Ibid.

30. Ibid., p. 89.

31. Collect for Christmas Eve and Christmas Day in J. Morley, *All Desires Known* (London: SPCK, 1992), p. 6.

32. J. Morley, 'The Faltering Words of Men' in M. Furlong (ed.), *Feminine in the Church* (London: SPCK, 1984), p. 64.

33. New York: Random Press, 1989.

34. For example, L. Byrne, *The Hidden Tradition* and *The Hidden Voice* (London: SPCK).

35. M. Warner, *Alone of All Her Sex* (London: Pan Books, 1990).

36. M. Katoppo, *Compassionate and Free* (Geneva: WCC, 1979), p. 17.

37. H. K. Chung, *Struggle to Be the Sun Again* (London: SCM, 1991), p. 75.

38. C. Mangan, 'Mary and Women' in J. Hyland (ed.), *Mary and the Churches* (Dublin: Veritas Publications, 1989), p. 105.

39. Marina Warner in the 1974 edition of *Alone of All Her Sex*, at least, believed Mary's power was inevitably in decline as fem-

inism gained power and Mary's patriarchal potency was exposed.

40. Quoted in Chung, op. cit., p. 80.
41. Quoted in Chung, op.cit., p. 81.
42. Katoppo, op.cit., p. 22.
43. Mapa, quoted in Chung, op.cit., p. 84.
44. Chung, op.cit., p. 82.
45. *The Alternative Service Book* (The Central Board of Finance of the Church of England, 1980), p. 10.
46. GS 859.
47. Morley, op. cit., p. 60.
48. *Hymns and Psalms* (Methodist Pub. Ho.), no. 104.
49. *Hymns and Psalms*, p. viii, though Morley is concerned that this suggests alterations are a sop to the particularly sensitive. See 'The Faltering Words of Men', p. 61.
50. *Hymns and Psalms*, p. ix.
51. GS 859, p. 3.
52. GS 859, p. 3.
53. GS 859, p. 4.
54. *Hymns and Psalms*, no. 16.
55. *Enemy of Apathy* (Glasgow: Wild Goose Publications, 1990), p. 115.
56. Wren, op. cit., p. 3.
57. C. Walker Bynam, *Jesus as Mother* (University of California Press, 1982), p. 140.
58. Quoted in A. Loades, *Searching for Lost Coins* (London: SPCK, 1987). See also GS 859, p. 59, where this prayer is adapted as a canticle for public worship.
59. J. Cotter, *Prayer at Night* (Sheffield: Cairns Publications, 1983), p. 42.
60. J. Morley, *All Desires Known* (London: SPCK, 1992), p. 91.
61. J. Morley, 'I Desire Her with My Whole Heart' in A. Loades (ed.), *Feminist Theology: A Reader* (London: SPCK, 1990), p. 162.
62. It should be noted that many women priests would not regard themselves as feminists, nor be interested in or committed to a feminist stance.

63. S. F. Parsons, 'Women and Ministerial Training' in E. Graham and M. Halsey (eds.), *Life Cycles* (London: SPCK, 1993), p. 205.

64. Ibid., p. 206.

65. *The Tablet*, 4 January 1997, p. 3.

66. Feminism is not alone in this.

67. P. Webb, *Where are the Women?* (London: Epworth Press, 1979), p. 1.

Further Reading

Beattie, T., *Rediscovering Mary* (Tunbridge Wells: Burns and Oates, 1995)

Borrowdale, A., *A Woman's Work* (London: SPCK, 1989)

Bynam, C. Walker, *Jesus as Mother* (University of California Press, 1982)

Byrne, L., *The Hidden Tradition* (London: SPCK, 1991)
Women Before God (London: SPCK, 1988)

Christ, C. P. and Plaskow, J., *Womanspirit Rising* (San Francisco: Harper and Row, 1979)

Chung, H. K., *Struggle to Be the Sun Again* (London: SCM, 1991)

Commission on Women Presbyters and the Church, *The Cry of the Beloved* (London: Methodist Publishing House, 1995)

Cotter, J., *Prayer at Night* (Sheffield: Cairns Publications, 1983)

Dowell, S. and Hurcombe, L., *Dispossessed Daughters of Eve* (London: SPCK, 1981)

Elwes, T. (ed.), *Women's Voices* (Marshall Pickering, 1992)

Fiorenza, E. S., *In Memory of Her* (London: SCM, 1983)
Searching the Scriptures Vol. I (London: SCM, 1993)

Friedan, B., *The Feminine Mystique* (London: Penguin, 1976)

Furlong, M. (ed.), *Feminine in the Church* (London: SPCK, 1984)

Graham, E. and Halsey, M. (eds.), *Life Cycles* (London: SPCK, 1993)

Graham, E., *Making the Difference* (London: Mowbray, 1995)

Gunew, S. (ed.), *Feminist Knowledge: Critique and Construct* (London: Routledge, 1990)

A Reader in Feminist Knowledge (London: Routledge, 1991)

Hampson, D., *Theology and Feminism* (Oxford: Basil Blackwell, 1990)

Hogan, L., *From Women's Experience to Feminist Theology* (Sheffield: Sheffield Academic Press, 1995)

Holloway, R. (ed.), *Who Needs Feminism?* (London: SPCK, 1991)

Isherwood, L. and McEwan, D. (eds.), *An A to Z of Feminist Theology* (Sheffield: Sheffield Academic Press, 1996)

Katoppo, M., *Compassionate and Free* (Geneva: WCC, 1979)

Lafferty, A., *Wives, Harlots and Concubines – Women in the Old Testament* (London: SPCK, 1990)

Loades, A., *Searching for Lost Coins* (London: SPCK, 1987)

(ed.), *Feminist Theology: A Reader* (London: SPCK, 1990)

Mangan, C., 'Mary and Women' in J. Hyland (ed.), *Mary and the Churches* (Dublin: Veritas Publications, 1989)

Moltmann-Wendel, E., *The Women Around Jesus* (London: SCM, 1982)

Moltmann-Wendel, E. and Moltmann, J., *God – His and Hers* (London: SCM, 1991)

Morley, J., *All Desires Known* (London: SPCK, 1992)

Pagels, E., *The Gnostic Gospels* (New York: Random Press, 1989)

Rowland, C., *Radical Christianity* (Cambridge: Polity Press, 1988)

Ruether, R., *Sexism and God-Talk* (London: SCM, 1983)

Slee, N., 'Parables and Women's Experience' in *MC* 26:2 (1984)

Trible, P., *Texts of Terror* (Philadelphia: Fortress Press, 1984)

Walker, A., *In Search of Our Mothers' Gardens* (London: The Women's Press, 1984)

Ward, H., Wild, J. and Morley, J. (eds.), *Celebrating Women* (London: SPCK, 1995)

Warner, M., *Alone of All Her Sex* (London: Pan Books, 1990)

Webb, P., *Where are the Women?* (London: Epworth Press, 1979)

Women's Guild/Panel on Doctrine, *The Motherhood of God* (Edinburgh: St Andrew's Press, 1984)

Wren, B., *What Language Shall I Borrow?* (London: SCM, 1989)